In memory of my beloved mother, Tara, the brightest star in the firmament, my guiding light

Whenever I am lost in the darkness, I look up, and I know I will find you, my shining star

EXPRESSIONS OF DIVINITY
MAHA KUMBH
2025

MEENAKSHI SINGH

BLOOMSBURY
NEW DELHI • LONDON • OXFORD • NEW YORK • SYDNEY

BLOOMSBURY INDIA
Bloomsbury Publishing India Pvt. Ltd
Second Floor, LSC Building No. 4, DDA Complex,
Pocket C – 6 & 7, Vasant Kunj,
New Delhi 110070

BLOOMSBURY, BLOOMSBURY QUEST and the Diana logo are
trademarks of Bloomsbury Publishing Plc

First published in India 2025

ISBN: 978-93-69524-65-5
2 4 6 8 10 9 7 5 3 1

Printed and bound in India by Thomson Press India Ltd

To find out more about our authors and books, visit
www.bloomsbury.com and sign up for our newsletters

CONTENTS

SANGAM: THE SACRED CONFLUENCE

PREFACE

From as far back as I remember, my life has been shaped by the Ganga, the Yamuna and perhaps even the Saraswati – that unseen, silent river that for me has stood for the hidden, the unknowable and the enigmatic self. Though I inhabit a modern, tech-driven world, I have always believed that behind tangible reality there is another reality that drives the visible world, like an unseen current shaping the visible shore. These rivers help remind me of this.

Another force that has guided me, just as surely, are my values, the ingrained ethos coursing through me: the cultural values planted deep into my consciousness by my family, my upbringing, my experiences and even my past lives. Even though my life's path has carried me far from those early environments, I have carried my innate values in my heart like a talisman that moors me to my roots. And now, in my middle years, I find myself drawn back, gathering what I can to pass on to my sons so that they too may know where they come from.

This book is dedicated to my mother, who planted and nurtured those ancient cultural values in my mind when I was a girl. It is also my gift as a mother to my two sons, Rudra and Ribhav, so that they may understand the traditions and the legacy they carry in them, consciously and subconsciously.

My late father, Shri R.B. Singh ji, was an officer with the Uttar Pradesh Police. He had a transferable job and somehow destiny – for I do not believe it was coincidence – stationed us close to either the Ganga or the Yamuna. Even after my marriage, the rivers never left my side. My husband, Rajeev Krishna, an IPS officer, too was posted in cities like Agra, Mathura, Fatehgarh, Aligarh, all riverine cities with the Ganga or the Yamuna coursing through them, as in the cities where I had spent my childhood days. Wherever life has led me, the rivers have always been there, a constant in the changing phases of my journey.

My earliest memories of the Ganga are from the time I lived for a few years at my parents' house in the Civil Lines of Allahabad. In those simpler days, before malls and multiplexes, an evening outing meant piling into our 1974 model Fiat car with my parents and siblings and heading down to Gangaji to enjoy the sunset and the cool breeze that wafted across the waters. The ghats would be quiet then, with just a smattering of families and sadhus. At dusk, when it was time for the Ganga arti and the temple priest began it, we would do our achaman, whisper our small prayers and set afloat our burning ghee diyas shaped like the palash leaves, watching them get carried down the river like a small galaxy of stars.

No visit to the Sangam was complete without a visit to the Bade Hanuman Ji Temple, where Bajrangbali lies resting on his back with his foot resting on Ahiravan, the defeated demon king of Pataal Lok. When my father was posted in Aligarh, on the banks of the Yamuna, I would often go to take darshan of the famous Devraha Baba, the 'ageless yogi' of Vrindavan. Devraha Baba lived in a hut built on a high wooden platform by the river. I had gone there once and complained to him about my small worries. He had smiled at me and said simply, 'Karm kaand hoga' – your deeds will carve your way. Then with a touch of his foot to my head, he had blessed me, and I had recited: 'Om Namoh Bhagvate Vasudeva' – I bow to Krishna, the Supreme Consciousness. His touch always reminded me of Hanuman ji at Sangam. To me, Hanuman has always been more than a deity – he is a childhood friend and an invisible protector walking alongside me through life.

In Allahabad, the Mauni Amavasya – the moonless night sacred to silence – was always spent on the banks of the Ganga. Since my father was with the police, we sometimes spent the nights in the large canvas tents erected on the banks of the river where the officers' families could stay. I remember how exciting it was for us children. At about 3.30 a.m., during the Brahma Muhurat, my mother and grandmother would wake us up – not with words, since speaking was forbidden during the Mauni Amavasya – by clanging spoons against a plate.

Before dawn, the sky would be a deep indigo, with the stars hanging low. In the winter night, the river would be enveloped in cold mist. Lamps would flicker on the ghats, with devotees moving about silently. We would walk down to the ghat and slip into the dark waters – an indescribable, magical feeling. The water would be cold and the night dark, yet these moments between night and morning were moments suspended between past and possibility.

During the Kumbh Mela in those years, I remember the smoky evenings where the ash-smeared sadhus contemplated by their smouldering dhunis and the pilgrims huddled by small fires. That mysterious, timeless world imprinted itself deeply within me. Perhaps it was the same yearning for timelessness that later drew me to create my first display of photographic works on the Taj Mahal in Delhi. Naturally, when a couple of years later, a once-in-a-lifetime opportunity in 144 years – the Maha Kumbh 2025 – came, I wanted to capture the eternity of those celestial moments. Through this book, I have tried to present my humble offerings of the expressions of divinity that Maha Kumbh 2025 was.

My gratitude to my brothers, Rameshwar Singh and Rajeshwar Singh, and my sister, Abha Singh, for sharing the blessed childhood we had near the Ganga and the Yamuna.

My respects to my mentor in photography, Lalit Rajora, for helping me navigate the world of photography with his patience, insight and guidance.

I acknowledge with gratitude all my family and friends, my fellow travellers in this temporal journey who have supported me as I move ahead in my quest to be one with the infinite.

I believe these rivers have blessed and protected us, intertwining their stories with the stories of our family. As the old Sanskrit saying goes:

|| नद्यः सन्तः पावयन्ति लोकान ||

Like saints, the rivers purify the world.

I feel chosen.
I feel blessed.
Om Shanti.

|| त्रिवेणी माधावं सोमं भारद्वाजं च वासुकीम्।
वन्दे अक्षयवटं शेषं प्रयागं तीर्थनायकम् ||

I bow to Triveni
(the confluence of the Ganga, the Yamuna and the Saraswati),
To Madhava (Lord Vishnu),
To Soma (Lord Shiva),
To Bharadvaja (the sage),
To Vasuki (the serpent king),
To the immortal Banyan tree (Akshayavat),
To Shesha (the cosmic serpent),
And to Prayag, the foremost among pilgrimage sites.

The tides of faith immersing in the liberating waters of the rivers Ganga, Yamuna and Saraswati at the Holy Sangam

In this land, it is believed that all existence is an expression of the divine. A stone, a tree, a snake, a cow, a monkey, an elephant, a bull – all these and more are worshipped as an embodiment of a deity; every river is a goddess, and every mountain and forest has a dwelling spirit. People greet each other with a 'namaste', which means 'I bow to the divine in you'. But it is more than that; it is humility, respect and the recognition of the divinity in every being. And so everything – the seen and the unseen – is rooted in the divine. Even death and destruction are part of the divine drama. In this land, it is believed that Creation is a vast, eternal tapestry, where every shining thread is spun from the spinning wheel of God.

And within this Creation there are some places that are much more than geographies. They are like cosmic portals or gateways – natural vortices of energy, where the sacred pulses through stone, water and air. These are not just landscapes – they are living mandalas, where the boundaries between the physical and the spiritual grow thin. Whether it is the confluence of rivers at Prayag, the twelve Jyotirlingas or mountains where sages once meditated – such spaces are stamped with an energy imprint that still vibrates with intention, devotion and presence. They are not made sacred by human intent but by a timeless current of cosmic alignment and a resonance that reverberates in a way that can be distinctly felt and experienced. And within those sacred geographies, there are also sacred timings. When the energy is at its most intense. When the veil between the temporal and the spiritual is at its most transparent.

The Kumbh Mela at Prayag is one such convergence – of not just rivers and pilgrims, but of time, space and planetary alignment. Held at the Triveni Sangam, where the Ganga, the Yamuna and the invisible Saraswati meet, the Kumbh unfolds during astrologically potent periods. At such times, the position of the planets mirrors the auspiciousness of the geographic latitudes. When Jupiter moves into Aquarius, and the Sun enters the constellation of Aries, for forty-five days in the month of Magh (January to February), every twelve years, the site becomes a living temple, supercharged by millennia of faith, ritual and longing. The air thickens with mantras, incense, dust and devotion, and at that particular time the rivers are said to carry not just water, but the possibility of liberation. It is there that karma dissolves, the past loses its weight and the soul remembers its origin.

Within those forty-five days, there are some days which are even more potent. It is said that on those days the rivers hold a heightened charge, a quiet power shaped by ancient rhythm and devotion. People come not only to wash away karma but also to feel part of the larger cosmic vibrations. All are drawn by a force older than memory. Millions move as one – sadhus, seekers, saints and ordinary souls – in a moment of collective transcendence. Each pilgrim emerges from the water feeling one with the universe.

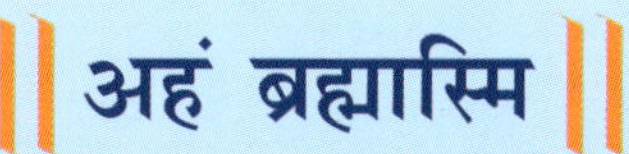

I am Brahman (the infinite reality).

Brihadaranyaka Upnishad, Adhyaya 1

BETWEEN RIVER AND SKY: MAPPING THE SHRINES AROUND THE SANGAM

|| यानि तीर्थानि पुण्यान्याकाशेऽन्तरदिवि स्थिताः
तानि सर्वाणि गङ्गायां प्रयागे च विशेषतः ||

All the holy pilgrimage sites that exist in the heavens,
Or between heaven and earth,
Are found in the Ganga, especially at Prayag.

from the *Prayāga Māhātmya* in the Matsya Purana
(between 250 and 500 CE)

The sacred landscape surrounding the Triveni Sangam in Prayag is alive with temples and shrines that echo centuries of myths and devotion. Here architecture is not just built form, but a vessel for stories, rituals and the timeless pulse of the divine. These sites make a tapestry of devotion that extends the sanctity of the Sangam well beyond the meeting of the rivers.

BADE HANUMAN JI TEMPLE

Tucked away near the Sangam is the Bade Hanuman Ji Temple, with a twenty-foot-long idol of a reclining Lord Hanuman, said to be one of its kind in the world. During the monsoon, when the Ganga swells and rises, the water often enters the chamber, partially submerging the deity. Far from being seen as a concern, this natural occurrence is embraced by devotees, who believe it symbolizes Hanuman's humility and surrender to divine will, allowing himself to be sanctified by the river goddess. It is believed that during the Mahabharata era (fourth century BCE to fourth century CE), when Arjun was travelling with Lord Krishna, he requested Hanuman to sit in his chariot. After the war ended, Hanuman adopted a resting posture, thereby inspiring idols of Hanuman in a reclining posture. In yet another story, Suryadev told Hanuman that Ram, the son of King Dasharath of Ayodhya and a descendant of his dynasty, had been exiled along with his brother Laxman and wife, Sita, due to destiny's consequences. He instructed Hanuman to ensure that they did not face any difficulties in the forest and that no demon could harm them. After listening to Surya God, Hanuman left for Ayodhya. However, God thought that if Hanuman killed all the demons himself, the purpose of his incarnation would be lost. So he ordered Maya, the goddess of illusion, to put Hanuman into a deep sleep. Following the divine command, Maya set out in the direction from which Hanuman was coming. By the time Hanuman reached the banks of the Ganga, the sun had already set. He bowed to Mother Ganga and, believing that rivers should not be crossed at night, decided to spend the night on its bank, and so the idol of a resting Hanuman came to be.

PATAALPURI

In the shadows of the ramparts of the Allahabad Fort at the Sangam lies one of India's most mysterious and occult sites – the Pataalpuri Temple. Generations of sages and seekers have seen it as a secret, mystical passage to the underworld – Pataal Lok. In Hindu cosmology, Pataal Lok (or Pataal) refers to one of the seven netherworlds, a subterranean realm that exists beneath the earth. These aren't physical locations, rather they are metaphysical planes, with their own frequencies, beings and energy dynamics. The netherworld is not hell in the way Western traditions describe it, but rather a complex, vibrant world with its own purpose and inhabitants. In fact, the Puranas describe it as a realm of incredible beauty, filled with palaces, treasures and advanced beings. It is ruled by nagas, serpent beings of deep and coiled wisdom, and asuras, who are not necessarily evil but are opposed to or different from the devas. Vasuki, the serpent king who helped churn the Kshirsagar, was called up from Pataal Lok.

Spiritually, Pataal Lok represents the subconscious mind, with its hidden desires, latent energies and layers of karma. Just as the cosmos has layers, we too have layers to our being. Visiting a subterranean shrine like the Pataalpuri Temple symbolizes a descent into the primal self.

The Pataalpuri Temple is believed to predate recorded history. Scholars suggest that the original shrine – possibly just a cave or a sacred underground chamber – was in use during the Vedic period (roughly 1500 BCE–500 BCE). It also finds mention in various scriptures and travel accounts as a site of spiritual power, where gods and rishis were once believed to descend to.

Descriptions of an underground temple at Prayag are found in the Mahabharata and the Puranas. In the centuries that followed, as the Triveni Sangam gained fame, the area became one of Hinduism's holiest pilgrimage sites.

Entering the temple is like stepping through time. The air is cooler, denser, carrying the faint scent of oil lamps and old stone. Carvings of deities line the subterranean walls, weathered by time and anointed with vermillion and sandalwood paste.

Shiv Temple near Arail Ghat

The Mankameshwar temple is a powerful shrine dedicated to Lord Shiva. The name Mankameshwar means 'fulfiller of desires'. So why is Shiva, the supreme Yogi, the ash-smeared ascetic, the one immersed in samadhi, the renunciate who is beyond desire – why is such a one worshipped as Mankameshwar, 'the fulfiller of desires'? The answer lies in the layered nature of Shiva's identity and in the way Bhakti traditions interact with metaphysical truths.

Also, in many yogic and tantric philosophies, desire is not shunned – it is recognized as the starting point of the spiritual journey. Shiva grants not just what he is asked, but often what is needed – such as insight, detachment or clarity. Thus, the Mankameshwar temple becomes a bridge between the worldly and the transcendental. Local legend weaves this temple into the epic of the Ramayana, suggesting that it was Lord Ram himself who consecrated the Shiva lingam here, honouring Sita's wish to offer prayers to Shiva before their journey into the forest.

Benimadhav temple is yet another powerful site for prayers and rituals, among other places of reverence in Prayag.

Shivalaya Park

SARASWATI KOOP

Saraswati Koop, where the mythical Saraswati river flows towards the Sangam

ALOPI DEVI

Another site of deep devotion is in the quiet neighbourhood of Alopibagh, where the narrow lanes open into the Alopi Devi Temple. At the sanctum's centre rests a simple wooden palanquin, or doli, draped in red and gold, worshipped as Alopi Devi – the 'disappearing goddess'. According to legend, this is where the last fragment of Goddess Sati's body fell, as Lord Shiva, consumed by grief, wandered across the world carrying her charred remains. Each location where a part of her body fell became a Shakti Peetha – a highly charged site of the Divine Feminine. While Prayag is not listed in the most common classical lists of Shakti Peethas mentioned in the Kalika Purana or the Devi Bhagavata Purana, local and tantric traditions recognize the Alopi Temple as a potent site of Shakti, where the goddess is worshipped as formless. Here, the goddess is not shaped in stone or metal – she is presence without form, power without image. To bow at Alopi Devi's shrine is to revere the invisible, to sense divinity not in icons but in mystery and memory.

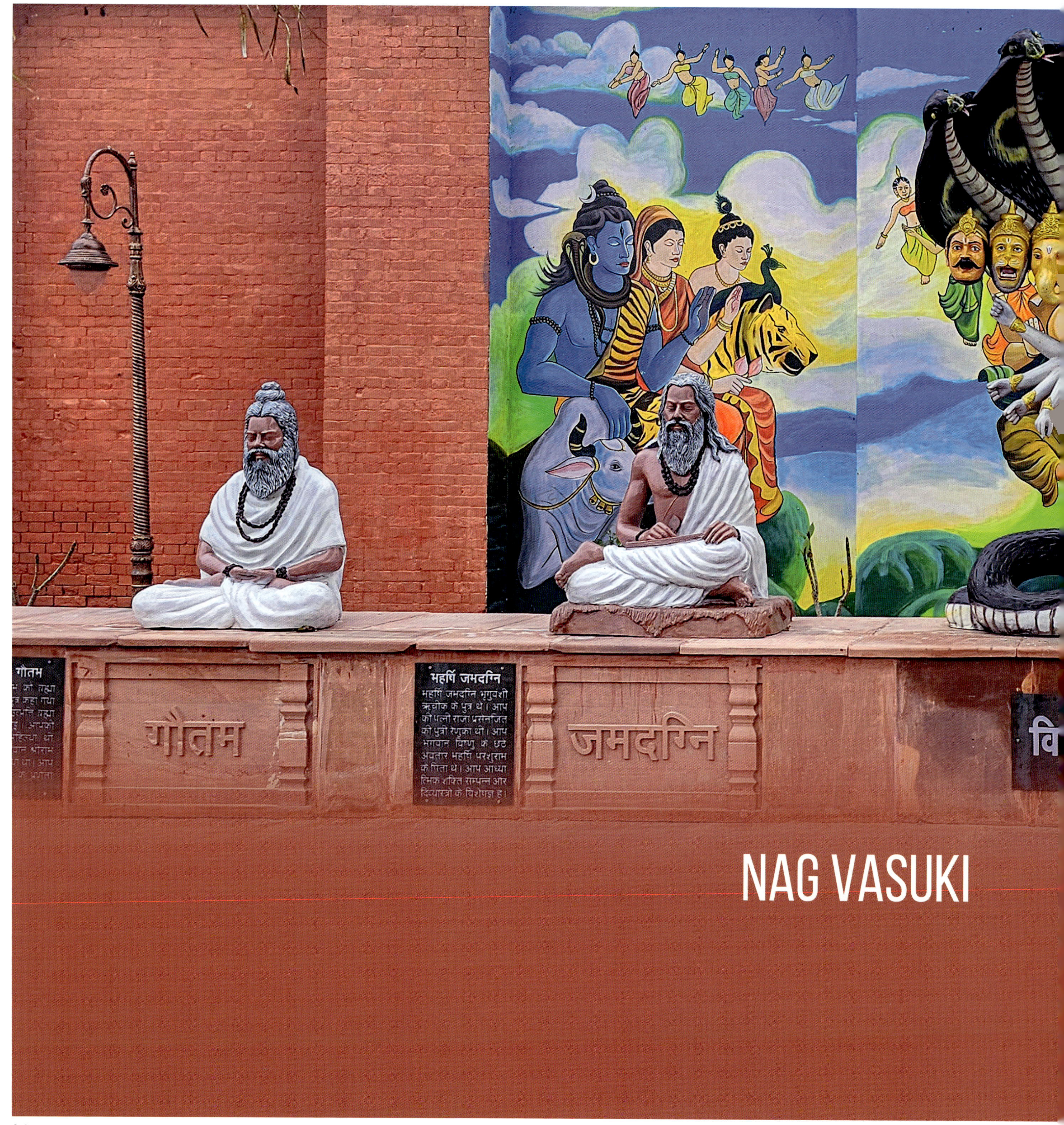
गौतम
गौतम
महर्षि जमदग्नि
महर्षि जमदग्नि भृगुवंशी ऋचीक के पुत्र थे। आप की पत्नी राजा प्रसेनजित की पुत्री रेणुका थी। आप भगवान विष्णु के छठे अवतार महर्षि परशुराम के पिता थे। आप आध्यात्मिक शक्ति सम्पन्न और दिव्यास्त्रों के विशेषज्ञ हैं।
जमदग्नि

NAG VASUKI

Nag Vasuki is one of the most revered serpent deities in Hinduism and is believed to reside in Pataal Lok, the netherworld. In Samudra Manthan, wrapped around Mount Mandara, he served as the churning rope.

Considered to be the brother of Shesha Nag, the serpent on whom Lord Vishnu rests, Vasuki is deeply revered when depicted coiled around Lord Shiva's neck.

Vasuki's presence in Hindu mythology highlights the deep connection between nature, spirituality and divine protection. Naga Sadhus revere Vasuki as one of their spiritual protectors of cosmic balance.

In Chinese and Japanese mythology, Vasuki is revered as one of the eight great dragon kings.

दान पात्र

AKSHAYAVAT

At the heart of this sacred hollow stands something even older than the stones – the Akshayavat, or 'the Indestructible Banyan Tree'. Gnarled and modest in appearance, it does not flaunt its age or power; its significance echoes through centuries of mythology. Legend holds that during Pralaya – the great cosmic flood – the sage Markandeya floated alone on the infinite waters, clinging to nothingness. Then, out of that endless sea, he saw a lone banyan tree standing firm, untouched. Upon one of its leaves lay an infant – Lord Vishnu himself, serene and smiling, symbolizing the eternal nature of life. That banyan tree, many believe, is the immortal tree of heaven, Akshayavat, which in Prayagraj once covered an area of five yojana with its one hundred branches, as described in the Prayag Mahatmya Shatadhyayi, which glorifies the grace of the city.

Akshayavat of Prayag: The Atharvaveda assumed the tree as Brahmanda Vriksha, a tree covering the whole universe from space to the sky to the land. Further, the sacred text of Matsya Purana describes Akshayavat as an embodiment of Lord Shiva himself. Merely the sight of the sacred tree would bring the benefit of salvation to Hindus, as it is located on the north bank of the river Yamuna and on the eastern bank of the river Ganga. Padma Purana further identifies the place of the holy bath as the river confluence where the streams follow its direction towards the west. The Matsya Purana refers to the immortality of the tree when the twelve solar powers in the universe (Dwadasha Aditya) destroy the entire universe, leaving only the Akshayavat tree at Prayag remaining.

Local lore adds its own flavour. Elders in Prayag often speak of how, during especially intense monsoons, when the Ganga threatens to breach her banks, the tree is the bellwether: 'Watch,' they say, 'if even a leaf falls, all will not be well.' But the tree has never shed. It is called 'Akshaya' for a reason – eternal, undiminished.

हरिद्वारे कुम्भयोगो मेषार्के कुम्भगे गुरौ
प्रयागे मेषसंस्थेज्ये मकरस्थे दिवाकरे ॥
उज्जयिन्यां च मेषार्के सिंहस्थे च बृहस्पतौ।
सिंहस्थितेज्ये सिंहार्के नाशिके गौतमीतटे॥
सुधाबिन्दुविनिक्षेपात् कुम्भपर्वेति विश्रुतम्॥

When Jupiter enters Aquarius and the Sun enters Aries, the Kumbh Mela will be held on the banks of the Ganga in Haridwar. When the Sun is in Capricorn and Jupiter is in Aries, the Kumbh will take place in Prayagraj. If Jupiter is in Leo and the Sun is in Aries, the Kumbh will be held on the banks of the Shipra in Ujjain. When both Jupiter and the Sun are in Leo, the Kumbh will be organized on the banks of the Godavari in Nashik.

Traditional astrological formulation
cited in religious and astrological texts

WHAT THE RIVERS REMEMBER: A HISTORY OF THE KUMBH FROM MYTHOLOGY TO MASS MOVEMENT

Kumbh has deep scriptural and mythological roots. There are references to it in Vedic texts, Puranas and epics like the Ramayana and the Mahabharata, explaining its cosmic significance. The concept of sacred rivers, ritual bathing and amrit, the nectar of immortality, are interwoven with the core of our scriptural history, passed down over thousands of years via oral and written texts. The essence of Kumbh, ever since the drops of amrit spilled on the four sacred sites of Kumbh, has coursed through the civilizational veins of India for centuries. The Rigveda (Mandala 10.136) describes sages and divine beings purifying themselves in sacred rivers. The Yajurveda (Taittirya Samhita 7.4.8.3) highlights the importance of ritual baths in holy rivers for spiritual cleansing. The Atharvaveda (19.6, 19.7) refers to amrit and its role in granting immortality.

In Valmiki's Ramayana, the churning of the ocean appears in Bala Kanda, Chapter 45. Mankameshwar Tirtha Yatra Parva (Vana Parva, Chapters 83–84) of the Mahabharata describes the sacredness of Prayagraj and the confluence of the Ganga, the Yamuna and the Saraswati (Triveni Sangam). Shanti Parva (Chapter 22) recommends ritual bathing in holy rivers to wash away sins. Harivamsa (Appendix to Mahabharata, Chapter 19) describes the celestial drops of amrit falling at Kumbh locations.

The Puranas, composed between the third century BCE and eighth century CE, provide the mythological foundations of Kumbh Mela, especially the legend of Samudra Manthan. Key texts that describe the churning of the ocean by gods (devas) and demons (asuras) include Bhagavata Purana (Skanda 8, Adhyaya 5–8), Vayu Purana (Chapter 192) and Padma Purana (Brahma Kanda, Chapters 89–90). It is also mentioned in the Ramayana's Uttara Kanda (Chapters 231–233). During this episode, drops of amrit fell at four places – Prayagraj, Haridwar, Ujjain, Nashik – where Kumbh Mela is held. Matsya Purana (Chapters 100–102) recommends bathing in scared rivers during specific planetary alignments for liberation from sins and highlights Prayagraj as the most sacred pilgrimage site. Agni Purana (Chapters 28–30) describes the importance of taking a dip in the Ganga and other holy rivers during auspicious times. Brahmanda Purana lists the Kumbh locations and their significance for attaining moksha (liberation). It also discusses the importance of akharas (monastic orders in Kumbh). Padma Purana (Chapter 127) explains the rituals of bathing and doing charity during Kumbh and their spiritual benefits. Bhavishya Purana outlines astrological calculations that determine the Kumbh dates.

The Kumbh has fascinated travellers, scholars and spiritual seekers for centuries.

But it is probably the philosopher-saint Adi Shankaracharya who can be credited with transforming the Kumbh into the pan-Indian extravaganza that it is today. By the eighth century CE, India was a mosaic of belief systems – Buddhism, Jainism, tribal worship and varied Vedic schools – all flourishing, but sometimes in conflict with one another.

To promote religious cohesion, Shankaracharya encouraged sadhus, renunciates and seekers to gather at specific intervals, particularly during auspicious planetary alignments, to discuss philosophy, renew their spiritual vows and demonstrate dharma to the public. This vision planted the seeds of what would become the tradition of Kumbh Mela.

He established and formalized the akhara system and set up a powerful network of mutths (monasteries), which over time evolved into thirteen akharas in three main streams: Shaiv, Vaishnav and Udaseen. These thirteen akharas are Juna Akhara, Niranjani Akhara, Mahanirvani Akhara, Atal Akhara, Ahwan Akhara, Nirmohi Akhara, Anand Akhara, Panchgani Akhara, Nagpanthi Gorakhnath Akhara, Vaishnav Akhara, Udaseen Panchayati Bada Akhara, Udaseen Naya Akhara and Nirmal Panchayati Akhara. These akharas and other ascetic orders – each with distinct practices, but united under the spiritual umbrella of the Vedas – began assembling at the Kumbh, using it as a platform to debate, teach, initiate disciples and even settle disputes. What had once been a spontaneous religious bath now evolved into a structured, cyclic, spiritual parliament, with the Shahi Snan (royal bath) becoming both a ritual of purification and a political assertion of spiritual authority, and thus a scattered ritual observance transformed into a vast, collective pilgrimage that unified India's diverse sects, saints and seekers.

In *A Record of Buddhistic Kingdoms*, Faxian, one of the earliest and most prominent Chinese travellers who recorded his experiences and impressions, describes the religious landscape of fifth-century India in great detail. He emphasizes the sacred importance of rivers and their centrality in religious observances.

Xuanzang, another prominent Chinese traveller, visited India two centuries after Faxian and documented the grand religious gatherings at Prayagraj, possibly an early form of the Kumbh. Scholars posit that the Puranas were given their present form during the reign of the Guptas (between 400 and 600 CE), which lends credence to this hypothesis. Xuanzang records that the emperor distributed his wealth at these assemblies and that philosophical discussions were held at the confluence.

From this spiritual framework, the Kumbh grew. Al-Biruni, the renowned Persian scholar and keen observer of Indian culture, wrote extensively about the Indian practice of pilgrimage and religious festivals. He wrote about the performance of rituals by a large number of people at this confluence who were driven by the belief that such acts would cleanse them of sins and bring spiritual liberation. The link between these gatherings and the modern-day Kumbh is undeniable.

View of the Allahabad Fort, built in 1583, from the Yamuna River

In his seminal work *Kitab-ul-Hind*, Al-Biruni wrote about the reverence in which Indians held their rivers, particularly the Ganga, which he described as the lifeline of spiritual and cultural identity. His accounts offer an outsider's perspective, which becomes especially valuable since it captures the scale and fervour of these events without the lens of local tradition, offering a near anthropological record of eleventh-century India.

Over the centuries, kings began to patronize the Mela, not only for religious merit but also to align with the moral authority of sadhus. In time, the Mela also became a major economic and commercial hub, drawing merchants from across India and from Central Asia, Persia, Tibet and beyond. Despite being Islamic rulers in a largely Hindu land, the Mughals, especially Akbar and Jahangir, demonstrated a pragmatic, sometimes reverent, approach to the Kumbh Mela.

When time pauses to bow before the sacred:
An estimated 76.1 million devotees took the holy dip on the auspicious day of Mauni Amavasya on 29 January 2025

CHANGING ROOM

The six main days in the quest for salvation: Pausha Purnima, 13 January; Makar Sankranti, 14 January; Mauni Amavasya, 29 January; Basant Panchami, 3 February; Magha Purnima, 12 February; Mahashivratri, 26 February

From an adolescent to an ascetic

The akharas began to assume a more militant and organized structure – not just as spiritual communities, but also as defenders of dharma – during the Mughal period. Ascetics, particularly Naga sadhus, began to practise martial arts and carry arms. The Mughal court, while wary, often chose to negotiate with these powerful sects rather than confront them directly. In many ways, the coexistence of Mughal power and the sadhu tradition at the Kumbh reflects the larger paradox of the Indian subcontinent – a land where statecraft and spirituality have not collided but have coexisted, each shaping the other.

Abu'l Fazl in *Ain-i-Akbari* mentions Emperor Akbar's interest in Prayagraj's religious gatherings and the fort he built near Triveni Sangam. Mughal era records in *Tabaqat-e-Akbari*, which provide interesting references to the religious bathing festival, are of special importance as they are not mythological.

The seventeenth-century French traveller Jean-Baptiste Tavernier described the massive scale of Kumbh in those times.

By the time the British arrived in India in the late eighteenth century, the Kumbh Mela was an institution. In many ways, the Kumbh Mela served as a pre-modern globalization node, where faith and commerce met under the open sky. The first documented British analysis of Kumbh Mela dates to 1796, when Major General Thomas Hardwick compiled a comprehensive report on the Haridwar Kumbh, marking the beginning of the colonial administration's involvement in Kumbh.

Robert Montgomery Martin, a British civil servant, provided a vivid description of the Kumbh Mela at Haridwar in his 1858 book *The Indian Empire*:

> The visitors at the fair included people from a number of races and climes. Along with priests, soldiers, and religious mendicants, the fair had horse traders from Bukhara, Kabul, Turkistan as well as Arabs and Persians. The festival had roadside merchants of food grains, confectioners, clothes, toys and other items. Thousands of pilgrims in every form of transport as well as on foot marched to the pilgrimage site, dressed in colourful costumes, some without clothes, occasionally shouting 'Mahadeo Bol' and 'Bol, Bol' together. At night the riverbanks and camps illuminated with oil lamps, fireworks burst over the river, and innumerable floating lamps set by the pilgrims drifted downstream of the river.

Colonial records and travelogues offer vivid snapshots of the Kumbh's mercantile and spiritual energy. European painters, photographers and travel writers often viewed the Kumbh through an Oriental lens.

In 1897, Mark Twain attended the Kumbh Mela and was struck by the devotion and endurance of the pilgrim. He wrote in *Following the Equator*:

> It is wonderful, the power of a faith like that, that can make multitudes upon multitudes of the old and weak and the young and frail enter without hesitation or complaint upon such incredible journeys and endure the resultant miseries without repining.

In the eyes of the colonial state, the Kumbh was not a festival – it was a wild, ungoverned organism, and potentially a site of sedition and disease. Despite their suspicion, the British did not ban the Kumbh. They regulated it, mapped it, sanitized it and inadvertently formalized it. The colonial period transformed the Kumbh from a self-regulated river ritual into a semi-bureaucratic megaevent – complete with permits, medical tents, revenue charts and security grids.

कलशस्य मुखे विष्णुः कण्ठे रुद्रः समाश्रितः।
मूले तस्य स्थितो ब्रह्मा मधये मातृगणाः स्मृताः
कुक्षौ तु सागराः सर्वे सप्तद्वीपा वसुन्धारा।
ऋग्वेदोऽथ यजुर्वेदः सामवेदो ह्यथर्वणः।
अङ्गैश्च सहिताः सर्वे कलशं तु समाश्रिताः

Lord Vishnu resides at the mouth of the Kalash, Lord Rudra at its neck and Lord Brahma at its base.

All Mother Goddesses dwell in its middle part.
The oceans, the seven islands, and the entire earth are present in its womb.

The four Vedas – Rigveda, Yajurveda, Samaveda and Atharvaveda – along with all their branches,
are also established within the Kalash.

Kalasha Sthapana (कलश स्थापना),
a foundational ritual in Hindu ceremonies

AMRIT KALASH

Cultures around the world have myths centred on an elixir that grants immortality, wisdom or spiritual power. In Hinduism, this is amrit, the nectar that emerged from the churning of the cosmic ocean. In Greek mythology, the gods consumed ambrosia to maintain their immortality – forbidden to mortals. Chinese Taoist traditions speak of an elixir of immortality, pursued by sages and guarded by divine beings. In Norse mythology, the Mead of Poetry grants not eternal life but eternal wisdom and inspiration. This mead was stolen by Odin from the giants. The Epic of Gilgamesh from ancient Mesopotamia features a Plant of Life, which has the power to grant eternal youth. In Zoroastrianism, Haoma is a sacred drink that offers spiritual vitality and a connection to the divine. In Christian and Arthurian legend, the Holy Grail represents divine sustenance and eternal life, but only for the worthy. Across these traditions, the idea remains constant: immortality is a sacred gift, hidden, protected and accessible only through divine favour or inner purity.

The Kalasha Sthapana shloka portrays the Amrit (water of immortality) Kalash (pot) as a microcosm of the universe, containing deities, scriptures and elements of creation. Puranic texts such as the Bhagavata Purana (Canto 8), Vishnu Purana and Padma Purana describe a time in the early cycles of creation when even the devas were not immortal. Devas and asuras are considered offspring of the sisters Aditi and Diti, both married to Sage Kashyap, representing the eternal binaries of good and evil, order and chaos, maintaining the cosmic balance. Weakened by a curse

TRACING THE ORIGINS OF THE KUMBH

इमं मे ग्गि यमुने सरस्वति शुतुद्रि स्तोमं सचता परुष्ण्या।
असिक्न्या मरुद्वृधो वितस्तयार्जीकीये श्रृणुह्या सुवर्गे

O Ganga, Yamuna, Sarasvati,
Shutudri, together with Parushni,
Hear my praise, O Asikni, Marudvridha, Vitasta,
With Arjikiya, listen to me from the heavenly realm.

Hymn from Rigveda (10.75.5)

Aarti at the Triveni

of the sage Durvasa and desperate to reclaim their strength, the devas approached Lord Vishnu, seeking guidance. Lord Vishnu, Preserver of the Cosmos, advised an alliance with their rivals, the asuras, to undertake the churning of the cosmic ocean, the Kshirsagar, to extract amrit, the nectar of immortality.

Together, the devas and asuras uprooted the sacred Mount Mandara to use as a churning rod, and they enlisted the cosmic serpent Vasuki as the rope. With the devas pulling from one side and the asuras from the other, the ocean was churned – a vast, metaphysical act of creation and tension. This act, known as Samudra Manthan, symbolizes a deeper cosmic process – the churning of latent cosmic potential to bring forth creation, wisdom and the hidden gifts of existence. From this churning, fourteen divine treasures rose to the surface of the ocean – Kamadhenu, the wish-fulfilling cow; Airavata, the celestial elephant; Lakshmi, the goddess of wealth; the Moon; Kaustubha, the gem that would adorn Vishnu's chest; the Parijata tree; and so on, until finally, the most precious of all, Dhanvantri emerged holding amrit.

Not all that emerged from the churning was benevolent. The very first thing to rise from the depths of the ocean was Halahala, a highly toxic, corrosive poison, so potent that its fumes alone could destroy all life in the three worlds. Halahala symbolizes the destruction and suffering that are byproducts of transformation, whether spiritual, personal or cosmic.

Terrified, the asuras and devas turned to Shiva, Lord of Destruction, for help. Shiva gathered the Halahala as it rose to the surface, scooping it into his palms, and swallowed it. Parvati, his wife, placed her hand around Shiva's neck to prevent the poison from spreading in his body. As a result, Shiva's throat turned blue, earning him the name Neelkanth, 'the blue-throated one'. The symbolism here is beautiful. In Tantra and Shaiva philosophy, Shiva is pure consciousness and Parvati (or Shakti) is the creative, stabilizing energy, and together they maintain the cosmic balance, the mutual dependence of the divine masculine and feminine.

She ensures that the poison is held, neither swallowed (which would destroy him) nor released (which would destroy the world). It is a reminder that even divine strength needs grace to guide it.

During the struggle for the divine pot, four celestial beings – Brihaspati (Jupiter), Chandra (the Moon), Surya (the Sun) and Shani (Saturn) – were tasked with protecting it. The demons engaged in battle specifically with these four. Jayant, Indra's son, when running away from the asuras with the Kalash, spilled four drops of amrit at four places, where Kumbh is held.

To protect the amrit from the asuras and to deceive them, Vishnu assumed the form of Mohini, the divine enchantress. Vishnu's act seems like deception, but in Hindu philosophy, dharma is not always straightforward. When cosmic balance is at stake, the divine may take unconventional forms to restore it. Mohini represents Maya (illusion), wielded for righteous ends. Those ruled by ego (the asuras) are easily deceived by appearances, while those anchored in dharma (the devas) are able to see beyond outward form.

The Puranic accounts tell us that the river became a living channel of grace. In Hindu thought, rivers are not mere waterbodies but living goddesses. They are embodiments of divine flow, capable of transmitting sacred energy. Bathing during the Kumbh, especially on astrologically charged days, is more than ritual – it is a spiritual convergence, a chance to immerse in a current believed to carry the vibration of immortality itself.

The meeting of rivers mirrors the union of the individual soul (jivatma) with the universal soul (paramatma). Just as rivers lose their individual identities when they meet, the ego dissolves when the soul merges with the divine.

Havan on the bank of the river Ganga

TRIVENI: A TRIAD OF GODDESSES

गङ्गा यमुने सरस्वति शुतुद्रि स्तोमं सचता परुष्ण्या।
असिक्न्या मरुद्वृधो वितस्तया सरस्वत्या अर्णो नधीतमः॥

O Ganga, Yamuna, Sarasvati, Sutudri (Sutlej) and Parushni (Ravi),
With Asikni (Chenab), Marudvridha, and Vitasta (Jhelum),
May your collective praises flow abundantly,
O Sarasvati, bestow upon us your blessings.

Hymn from Rigveda (10.75.6)

Rivers in India have played a vital role in shaping settlements, agriculture, trade and pilgrimage routes for millennia. Rivers are deeply embedded within the cultural, spiritual and historical landscape of the subcontinent. From the earliest Vedic texts to contemporary ritual practice, rivers have been revered as living deities – especially female divinities – embodying fertility, purity and the flow of life itself. The Ganga, for instance, is of great significance in Hindu cosmology. Similarly, the Yamuna and the now-invisible Saraswati are venerated in scriptural literature and continue to hold theological significance. Rituals such as bathing, offering prayers and performing funerary rites by the riverbanks reflect these beliefs.

गङ्गां शरणं गच्छामि सर्वपापप्रणाशिनीम्।

I take refuge in Ganga, the destroyer of all sins.

Devotional verse composed in later
Hindu religious or liturgical tradition

Of the three, the Ganga is the holiest. She is wrapped in a hundred myths and folktales and occupies a central place in Hindu devotional life. Described in the Rigveda as a purifying and benevolent force, the Ganga is later personified in the epics and Puranas as Ganga Devi, a celestial being who descended on earth to absolve the sins of humanity. According to one of the most enduring myths, she was brought down from the heavens through the penance of King Bhagiratha and contained by Lord Shiva, who received her in his matted locks to soften her potentially destructive descent on earth. Beyond mythology, the Ganga has long functioned as a ritual axis for cremation rites, ancestral offerings (shraadh) and pilgrimages – from its source at Gaumukh in the Himalayas to its vast delta at Gangasagar in the Bay of Bengal. Despite environmental degradation in recent decades, the river remains a potent symbol of spiritual renewal, and at the Triveni Sangam, the sanctity of her presence is magnified.

For millennia, the banks of the Ganga have cradled some of the world's oldest and most enduring civilizations. The river nourished not just crops but philosophies – from the Vedas and Upanishads to the debates of Buddhist councils and Jain ascetics. Knowledge systems in astronomy, mathematics, medicine and metaphysics flourished along its meandering course, passed down through oral traditions and palm-leaf manuscripts. The Ganga was not merely a river – it was a moving university, a witness to the evolution of ideas.

In 1775, the French philosopher Voltaire wrote, 'I am convinced that everything has come down to us from the banks of the Ganges – astronomy, astrology, metempsychosis, etc. It is very important to note that some 2,500 years ago at the least, Pythagoras went from Samos to the Ganges to learn geometry.'

Indeed, it is widely held that Pythagoras, the Greek philosopher-mathematician famous for his eponymous theorem, travelled to the Ganga in the sixth century BCE to learn about the soul and other cosmic concepts from Brahmins. The similarities between Pythagorean doctrines and Indian upanishadic ideas are too striking to ignore.

Long before the rise of the Ganga-centred civilizations, the banks of the now-lost Saraswati River nurtured some of the earliest urban settlements in the Indian subcontinent. Archaeological finds from sites like Harappa, Mohenjo-daro and Rakhigarhi – many of which lie along what is believed to be the dry riverbed of the Saraswati – point to a mature culture that flourished between 2600 BCE and 1900 BCE.

Rigvedic hymns celebrate the Saraswati as the 'best of mothers, best of rivers, best of goddesses'. The river flows through a metaphysical as well as physical space. Whether the Saraswati dried due to tectonic shifts or climatic change, its cultural memory continued to flow, shaping Hindu civilization long after its waters vanished. The course of the river as described in the Rigveda points to it having once run through north-west India, from the Himalayas down through what is now Haryana and Rajasthan and into the Rann of Kutch, eventually emptying into the Arabian Sea. Its course has largely dried up, but satellite imagery and geological studies have traced paleochannels (ancient riverbeds) that are consistent with the descriptions in Vedic texts.

Nightlights at the cable-stayed New Yamuna Bridge
(Shyama Prasad Mukherjee Setu)

यत्र गंगा यमुना च सरस्वती च संगमः।
तत्र पुण्यं समुत्पन्नं मुक्ति ददाति निश्चलम्॥

Where the rivers Ganga, Yamuna, and Saraswati meet,
That place is supremely auspicious and grants unwavering liberation.

Matsya Purana and Padma Purana
(between 250 CE and 500 CE)

The story goes that Saraswati, upset by the wars and ego of humankind, chose to withdraw from the visible world, retreating into the underworld or Pataala and continuing to flow beneath the earth. At Prayag, she is believed to re-emerge subtly, joining the Ganga and the Yamuna at the Triveni Sangam, not in sight but in spirit.

The Yamuna has her own myths. She is the daughter of Surya, the sun god, and sister of Yama, the god of death. In the Vedic texts, she is mentioned sparingly compared to the Saraswati and the Ganga; but over time, her significance grew – especially through the Puranic and epic traditions. Flowing past ancient cities like Mathura, Vrindavan and Delhi, the Yamuna became deeply intertwined with the life and lores of Lord Krishna. In this role, she is not just a river but a stage – a witness to leela – divine play, love and liberation.

Historically, the Yamuna's fertile basin supported vibrant urban cultures and trade networks. The Indo-Gangetic plain, nourished by her waters, became a crucible for empires – from the Mauryas and the Guptas to the Delhi Sultanate and the Mughals. While the Ganga became a symbol of purity and salvation and the Saraswati of knowledge and mysticism, the Yamuna emerged as the river of intimate devotion – softer, more emotional, often feminine in metaphor. Over time, she came to embody the heart's yearning, flowing not just through lands but also the verses of poets, the strokes of miniature paintings and the passion of lovers.

|| इमं मे गङ्गे यमुने सरस्वति शुतुद्रि स्तोमं सचता परुष्ण्या।
असिक्न्या मरुद्वृधो वितस्तयार्जीकीये श्रृणुह्या सुवर्गे ||

गंगा, यमुना, सरस्वती, शुतुद्रि और अन्य नदियों की
महिमा को नमन करता हूँ, जो मोक्षदायिनी हैं

DHUNI AND DUST: SADHUS OF THE MAHA KUMBH

ज्ञेयः स नित्यसंन्यासी यो न द्वेष्टि न काङ्क्षति।
निर्द्वन्द्वो हि महाबाहो सुखं बन्धात् प्रमुच्यते

O mighty-armed one (Arjuna),
Know that person to be a true renunciate,
Who neither hates nor desires.
Indeed, one who is free from all dualities,
Is easily released from bondage.

Bhagavad Gita (Chapter 5, Verse 3)

आपो हिष्ठा मयोभुवस्ता न ऊर्जे दधातन।
महे रणाय चक्षसे॥

जल आनंददायक है, यह हमें शद्रि प्रदान करता है
और महान कार्यों में सहायता करता है।

- ऋग्वेद 10.9:1

The waters are indeed bringers of delight, may they grant us vigour and nourishment. For great radiance and clarity (of mind and bod

They arrive, covered in ashes, wrapped in animal skin and mystery. From snowbound caves of the Himalayas, from the burning ghats of Varanasi, from crumbling ashrams in towns with no addresses, from the forests of Madhya Pradesh and from the hidden hermitages of the South, they gather. Not by announcement, but by cosmic rhythm.

Naked, cloaked, saffron-robed, dreadlocked, tattooed, trident-bearing, chanting, meditating, they come in thousands, each one a walking riddle.

The Kumbh Mela is many things: a religious festival, a logistical marvel, a congregation of the devout – but its raw energy is embodied in the iconic sadhus. During the Kumbh, their hidden world becomes briefly visible. What is usually veiled in smoke and solitude steps boldly into the open, like a mountain revealing itself through mist.

To the uninitiated, they may appear theatrical and exotic – men daubed in ash, eyes ablaze, some stark naked in the winter dawn, others seated still as statues for hours. But behind each form is discipline and a lineage that goes back centuries. They are not beggars or 'mystics for show' – they are seekers, warriors, poets, philosophers, madmen and mirrors.

Who are these men and women who have walked away from family, flesh and identity? What drives a soul to choose hunger over comfort, silence over speech, death-in-life over the noise of the world? And in this vast churning of faith that is the Kumbh, what do they see that others miss?

hey flow.

|| यो वै तीर्थे स्नात्वा पापात् प्रमुच्यते स वै स्वर्गलोकमाप्नोति || अथर्ववेद 19.6.2

जो तीर्थों में स्नान करता है, वह पापों से मुक्त होकर स्वर्गलोक को प्राप्त करता है।

A devotee

Surrendering to the divine flow within

Of mantras and meditation

माघ मकर गति रवि जब होई। तीरथ पतिहिं आव सब कोई।।
देव मनुज किन्नर नर श्रेनी। सादर मज्जहिं सकल त्रिवेनी।।
पूजहिं माधव पद जल जाता। परसि अखयवटु हरषहिं गाता।।
भारद्वाज आश्रम अति पावन। परम रम्य मुनिवर मन भाव।।
वहाँ होड़ मुनि ऋषय समाजा। जाहिं जे मज्जन तीरथ राजा।।
ज्जहिं प्रात समेत उछाहा। कहहि परस्पर हरि गुन गाहा।।

Tulsidas in *Shri Ramcharitmanas* (Bala Kanda), 1574 CE

When the Sun enters the zodiac sign of Capricorn in the month of Magh, people from all directions gather at the sacred pilgrimage site.

Deities, humans, celestial beings and sages all respectfully take a dip in the holy confluence of the three rivers (the Ganga, the Yamuna and the Saraswati).

Devotees worship the sacred water of Lord Madhav's feet, and after touching the eternal banyan tree (Akhshayavat), they sing with joy.

The ashram of Sage Bharadwaj is pure, divine and enchanting, pleasing the hearts of sages. Great sages and ascetics gather there, and all proceed to bathe at the king of pilgrimages (Prayag). With enthusiasm, they immerse themselves at dawn and sing the glories of Lord Hari to one another.

Nearly a million kalpavasis (temporary residents) resided at the Mela premises from Pausha Purnima to Magha Purnima, practising austerity, devotion and self-purification

At the Kumbh, they do not just gather – they reign. They are not fringe figures here, they are the centre. And among them, the most visible and organized are the sadhus of the akharas. The akharas are ancient martial–spiritual orders that stretch back to a thousand years, each with its own history, parampara (guru lineage), ritual code and fierce identity.

The Juna, Niranjani, Mahanirvani, Atal, Bada Udaseen and Nirmal akhadas are not merely religious collectives, they are spiritual armies, forged in an era when sadhus carried swords and fought to defend temples and philosophy. Each akhada is a world in itself, with hierarchies, ceremonies and internal politics. During the Kumbh, their sprawling camps, lavishly decorated or starkly austere, become a theatre of mantra, debate, rituals and philosophical discourse. And, of course, of spectacle.

The naked Naga sadhus, with their ash-smeared bodies and wild eyes, belong to the warrior tradition of the Juna akhara. They march through the Kumbh like a living myth, wielding tridents and chillums, invoking Shiva with each step. Their Shahi Snan, the royal bath, is not just a ritual dip but a thunderous procession, part theatre, part trance and all power.

Akharas heading towards the Amrit Snan, the most important ritual of the Maha Kumbh

Not all sadhus are loud. Some sit quietly under canvas roofs, giving darshan, answering questions with riddles or softly chanting mantras. Others stare blankly into their dhuni fire, unmoving for hours. There are those who have chosen to stand on one leg or with an uplifted arm for years, and a few who have not slept prone for years.

These are not acts of self-torture but of tapasya. Tapasya are austerities and acts of extreme discipline that many sadhus voluntarily undertake to generate spiritual heat or 'taap' that will burn karma and help them attain mastery over their physical limitations. These spiritual practices are aimed at transcending the body, the ego and the ordinary mind. Some have taken vows of silence. These extreme practices are not about proving a point to the world. They are inward journeys; the outer austerity is just the surface of a deeper inner fire.

Nagas of the Shaiva akhara in cosmic bliss

|| यहि प्रकार भरि माघ नहाहिं, पुनि सब निज निज आश्रम जाहिं।
एक बार भरि मकर नहाए। सब मुनीस आश्रममन्ह सिघाए। ||

Shri Ramcharitmanas (Bala Kanda)

In this way, throughout the month of Magh, they take a holy dip and then return to their respective ashrams. Once, when the Sun enters Capricorn (Makar Rashi), all the sages and ascetics take a sacred bath and then swiftly return to their hermitages.

ज्ञेयः स नित्यसंन्यासी यो न द्वेष्टि न काङ् क्षति।
निर्द्वन्द्वो हि महाबाहो सुखं बन्धात्प्रमुच्यते।।

Bhagavad Gita (Chapter 5, Verse 3)

The karmyogis, who neither desire nor hate anything, should be considered always renounced.

Free from all dualities, they are easily liberated from the bonds of material energy.

|| त्रिवेणी संगमे स्नात्वा मुक्तिं प्राप्नोति मानवः ||

स्कंद पुराण, प्रयाग महात्मय

By bathing at the confluence of the three rivers (Triveni Sangam), a person attains liberation (moksha).

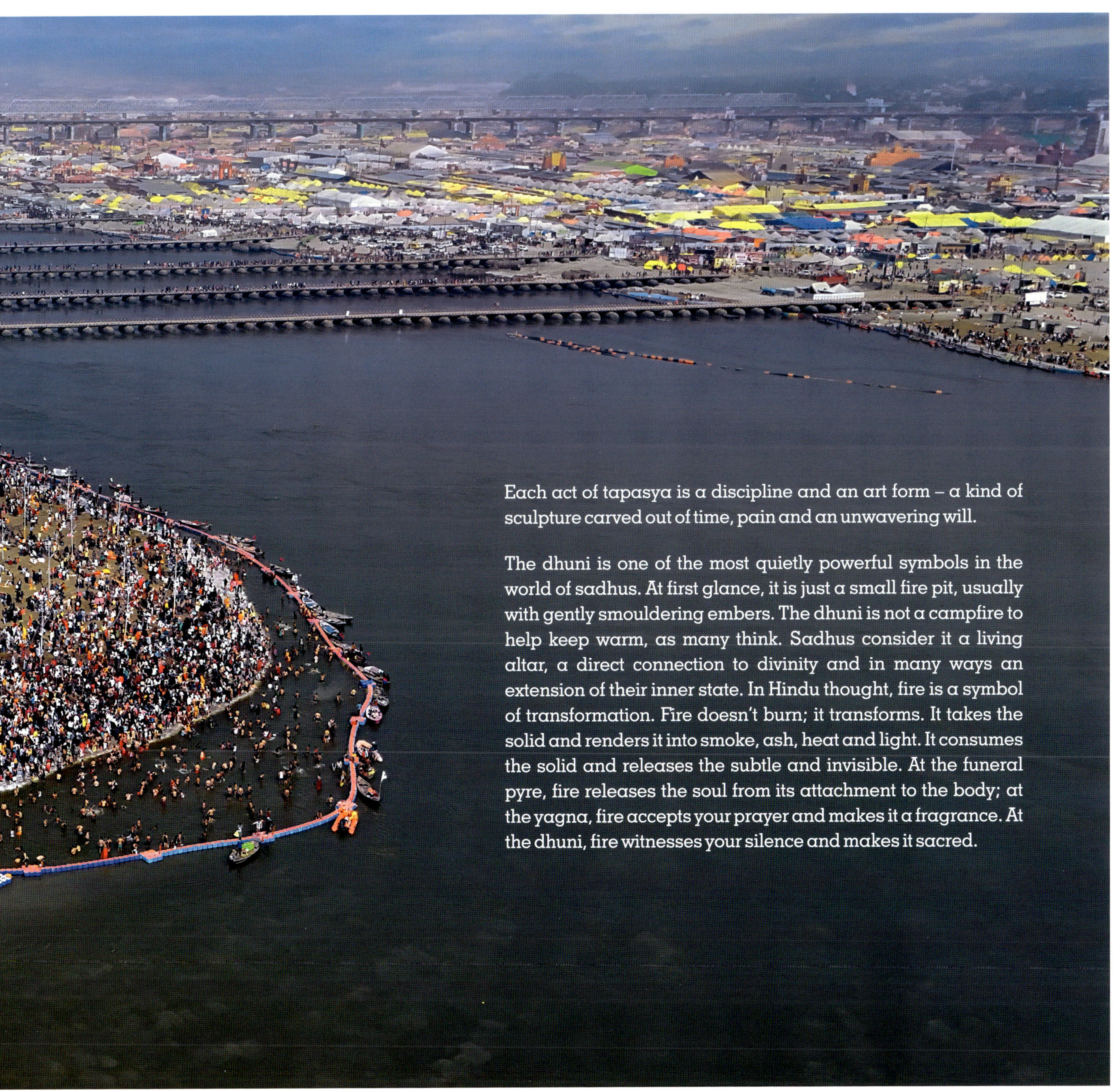

Each act of tapasya is a discipline and an art form – a kind of sculpture carved out of time, pain and an unwavering will.

The dhuni is one of the most quietly powerful symbols in the world of sadhus. At first glance, it is just a small fire pit, usually with gently smouldering embers. The dhuni is not a campfire to help keep warm, as many think. Sadhus consider it a living altar, a direct connection to divinity and in many ways an extension of their inner state. In Hindu thought, fire is a symbol of transformation. Fire doesn't burn; it transforms. It takes the solid and renders it into smoke, ash, heat and light. It consumes the solid and releases the subtle and invisible. At the funeral pyre, fire releases the soul from its attachment to the body; at the yagna, fire accepts your prayer and makes it a fragrance. At the dhuni, fire witnesses your silence and makes it sacred.

The defenders of faith

Eyes seeking the eternal

Fire is a living bridge between the physical and the spiritual. In Vedic tradition, Agni, the fire god, is the messenger. What you offer into the fire does not vanish. It is carried upward and transmitted. For many ascetics, especially Shaivite sadhus, the dhuni is directly connected to Shiva, the original renunciate. Shiva is said to reside in cremation grounds, surrounded by fire and ash. The dhuni becomes a symbolic yogic cremation ground, where the ego is meant to die and where awareness is reborn.

Sadhus say the fire 'speaks' to those who listen. Many sadhus begin and end their day at the dhuni. It becomes the axis on which their life revolves. Sadhus, especially Naga sadhus, smear their body with ash (vibhuti) from the dhuni, a symbol of impermanence and a reminder of death. Some sadhus, especially those in Shaivite akharas, smoke marijuana in a clay chillum by the dhuni. This is a ritual act of focus and detachment, not recreation. Unlike temples which are permanent and structured, the dhuni is a mobile temple, primal and alive. You can set it up wherever you go, making it the perfect spiritual anchor for a wandering sadhu.

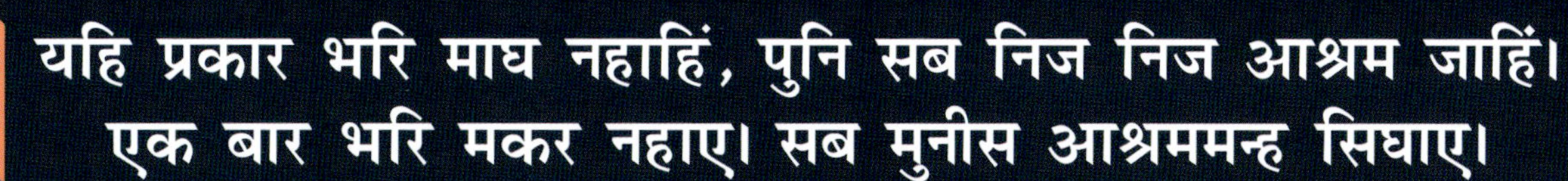

यहि प्रकार भरि माघ नहाहिं, पुनि सब निज निज आश्रम जाहिं।
एक बार भरि मकर नहाए। सब मुनीस आश्रममन्ह सिधाए।

Shri Ramcharitmanas (Bala Kanda)

In this way, throughout the month of Magh, they take a holy dip and then return to their respective ashrams.
When the Sun enters Capricorn (Makar Rashi), all the sages and ascetics take a sacred bath and swiftly return to their hermitages.

गङ्गा तव दर्शनात् मुक्तिर्जायते नृणाम्।
स्पर्शनात् पापनाशश्च जलपानात् परं सुखम्

The mere sight of the Ganga grants liberation, touching its water removes sins and drinking its water bestows supreme bliss.

Multitudes of faith coming together, making it the largest spiritual gathering in history with over 650 million pilgrims

JACK HEBNER AND DAVID OSBORN SAY IN *KUMBHA MELA: THE WORLD'S LARGEST ACT OF FAITH*

Pilgrims came by millions! Some arrived on overcrowded trains carrying five times the normal capacity. Some came by bus, some by car, some by ox-drawn carts and some rode horses, camels and even elephants. The rich and famous chartered private planes and helicopters; the less affluent came on foot, carrying their bedrolls and camping equipment in heavy bundles on their heads. Wave after wave, the pilgrims formed a veritable river of humanity that flowed onto the banks of the Ganges at Prayag (Allahabad) to celebrate the greatest spiritual festival ever held – the Kumbh Mela.

Performing sacred baths, charity and penance during the Kumbh grants the merits of a thousand Ashwamedha Yajnas without a doubt.

THE MAKING OF MAHA KUMBH 2025

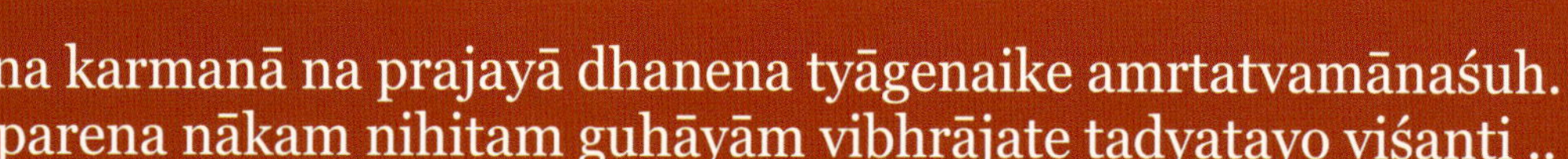

na karmanā na prajayā dhanena tyāgenaike amrtatvamānaśuh.
parena nākam nihitam guhāyām vibhrājate tadyatayo viśanti ..

Not by work, nor by progeny or by wealth, but by renunciation alone have some attained immortality. That (immortality) which is even beyond the heaven, is attained by the self-controlled renunciates (as the Self) shining in their heart.

Kaivalyopnishad, Verse 3
(approx. 1000 BCE)

Maha Kumbh 2025 was an event the likes of which has not been seen anywhere at any time. Around a tenth of the world's population gathered to pay homage and seek blessings in this festival of divinity over the course of two months. The scale, spiritual magnitude and logistical achievements that defined Maha Kumbh 2025 were indeed unimaginable and have no parallel anywhere in the world.

During the Kumbh, temporary settlements arise, forming an immense tent city, complete with roads, streetlights, tents, power lines, water tanks, police stations, food distribution centres, food stalls, medical camps and sanitation systems. An entire urban infrastructure appears where there was nothing. One of the most extraordinary aspects of the Kumbh Mela is the massive, self-contained tent city that rises to receive the millions of people it attracts. Built on the river's shifting floodplains – often in areas submerged for most of the year – this temporary city is constructed in a matter of weeks. It becomes home to millions of pilgrims, and then disappears as quickly as it came, leaving behind little more than footprints in the sand.

Around 665 million devotees, including over 1.5 million international tourists, nearly 1.9 million sages and Kalpvasis travelled from all over India and across the world to make the event a truly cosmopolitan gathering of believers.

The key bathing days saw the convergence of souls seeking salvation – the number of devotees attending the Kumbh on those days is an indicator of the faith of Indians. Official bulletins give the following figures about the participation of pilgrims on the bathing days:

January 13	Paush Purnima	15 million
January 14	Makar Sankranti (First Shahi Snan)	35 million
January 29	Mauni Amavasya (Second Shahi Snan)	76.1 million
February 3	Basant Panchami (Third Shahi Snan)	23.3 million
February 12	Maghi Purnima	20.1 million
February 26	Maha Shivratri	13.3 million

Devotees at the sanctum sanctorum of the Maha Kumbh 2025

Nightlights

Pontoon bridges serving as critical structures for the movement of millions

Seagulls: The birds of Maha Kumbh

On the threshold of divinity: One of the gates to enter the Maha Kumbh arena

View of the Kumbh city at night

View of the Naga Vasuki camp

Tent city: From the ephemeral to the eternal

Over 1,60,000 tents set up in the 4,000 hectare Mela area, divided into 25 sectors near Sangam, Arail and Phaphamau

Nearly 67,000 LED street lights, 2,000 solar lights for sustainable illumination and 4,50,000 new electricity connections

The foremost necessity for such a huge gathering is effective modes of transportation. For this, the Indian Railways executed an extraordinary transport operation involving over 15,000 trains, which catered to over 150 million pilgrims. This was supplemented by air travel, where historic improvements in infrastructure were undertaken in record time to cater to nearly 13,000 pilgrims daily in February. Lastly, road transport aided the remainder with thousands of special buses arriving and departing daily. For instance, around 4,500 buses were deployed on 26 February, the last day of the Kumbh.

Apart from the record-breaking transportation facilities, arrangements were made to provide medical facilities to the enormous influx of people. Both homeopathic and allopathic treatments were administered by the hospitals and clinics set up in the wake of the Kumbh. Over 4,50,000 pilgrims used the services of AYUSH centres along with emergency and specialized services; over a hundred ambulances and testing facilities for a myriad of tests were set up. This miracle of healthcare achieved the following: 3,70,000 pathology tests, more than 5,00,000 eye screenings and 10,000 daily consultations.

Over 50,000 police personnel, including over 4,000 home guards and paramilitary staff, exercised constant vigilance to ensure the smooth running of the Maha Kumbh. Nearly 2,750 AI-enabled CCTV cameras ensured real-time surveillance, and there were seventy police stations, of which fifty-seven were permanent. Additionally, twenty-three checkpoints ensured further security. Over 700 boats were deployed along with disaster response teams to address any mishap in the water. A dedicated cyber police station played a crucial role in safeguarding the Maha Kumbh, relying on the latest digital technology.

The efficient organization of the Maha Kumbh necessitated rapid infrastructural development to ensure that basic necessities were available. This push saw the creation of over 230 water ATMs, nearly 40,000 toilets and urinals, and a dedicated team of 22,000 sanitation workers. Around thirty pontoon bridges were built with over 3,000 pontoons. Over ninety base transceiver stations or BTS towers were constructed, ensuring internet coverage. Over 20,000 free meals were distributed daily, and 25,000 ration cards were issued during the duration of the Maha Kumbh.

Technology was leveraged effectively by employing the BHASHINI Platform, an AI-driven multilingual support platform capable of speaking in thirty languages, eleven Indian and nineteen international. Employment was generated for nearly 6,00,000 workers across sectors. The Confederation of All India Traders (CAIT) estimated that business of more than $25 billion was generated.

Apart from this, the Maha Kumbh highlighted the inclusivity and diversity of India through the participation of all thirteen akharas.

The effective management of an event which redefined what is meant by megaevents entails effective leadership. Regarding this, the guidance and vision of Prime Minister Shri Narendra Modi and Uttar Pradesh's Chief Minister Shri Yogi Adityanath was essential. Their close monitoring of the entire process to ensure it was conducted smoothly proved invaluable and set a very high benchmark for the future.

A CONFLUENCE OF SOULS: PILGRIMS OF THE MAHA KUMBH

प्रयागे संगमे पुण्ये स्नानदानजपादिभिः।
सर्वपापविनिर्मुक्तः शिवलोकं स गच्छति॥

By taking a holy bath, giving charity and chanting at Prayag Sangam, one is freed from sins and attains Shiva Loka.

Skanda Purana

आपो हिष्ठा मयोभुवस्ता न ऊर्जे दधातन।
महे रणाय चक्षसे॥

ऋग्वेद 10.9.1

At each Kumbh, millions of ordinary Indians head towards the confluence, on foot, in trains, by boats and now by cars and airplanes – a movement often described as a 'human tide'. The pilgrims themselves become like rivers, flowing from every corner of the land and converging towards a single point, the Sangam. During the Kumbh Mela, Prayag becomes a confluence of souls and of rivers. Just as rivers leave behind their origins and merge into something greater, the pilgrim sheds, at least temporarily, the boundaries of identity – caste, class, gender, occupation – and becomes part of a shared spiritual current. The human soul too can be likened to a river, moving, consciously or not, towards the infinite. The metaphor applies at multiple levels.

The idea of a ritual bath in a holy place is common to many belief systems. Our physical bodies are 72 per cent water. Taking a ritual dip in a sacred river is not just a cleansing but an act to enable the 72 per cent of our bodies that is water remember what it really is – a part of nature. Water constitutes a bridge between the physical and the spiritual. It carries memory, absorbs intention and offers renewal. The pilgrim who bathes at the Kumbh does so with the belief that in those few seconds of submersion, lifetimes of burden may be released and a new cycle may begin. There is also a communal dimension to the dip: the act of immersion happens with others, among others. It is not a solitary ascetic's pursuit but a mass sacrament. In a world increasingly defined by individualism, the Kumbh remains one of the few places where spiritual transformation is a collective act, performed for reasons both personal and eternal.

There is also a practical rhythm to daily life at the Kumbh, with devotees queuing for meals at community kitchens and securing spots for rest in crowded camps. They spend their days attending religious discourses (pravachans) led by saints and gurus, visiting akhara camps, listening to bhajans or engaging in personal rituals and prayers. Even amid the spiritual pursuit, there is logistical negotiation and cooperation. In this way, the Kumbh becomes not just a religious event but a temporary society, a sprawling spiritual and social landscape, held together by faith, patience and a kind of unspoken, collective choreography.

Turning to Parvati, Shiva had said, 'Moksha is easy, yet not easy at all. Without faith, it is impossible to attain. All the other pilgrims only indulged in a ritual. Ritual without true faith and pure intention is meaningless.'

Each Kumbh Mela sees the arrival of millions of people carrying with them their spiritual inheritance passed down through generations. They come not to attend 'The Greatest Show on Earth', as proclaimed by the UP Tourism hoardings. To them, a purifying dip at the Sangam is an article of faith, not a performance.

There is a prominent symbolism inherent in the phenomenon of temporary city, which comes up with the commencement of the Maha Kumbh and disappears with its closing on Mahashivratri. In Hindu philosophy, the material world is maya – a fleeting illusion, a passing show. The Kumbh's temporary city embodies this idea. It appears vast, and seemingly permanent, but everyone there knows that it will be gone in a matter of days. The very ground may vanish under the river once the waters return. This impermanence is not a flaw – it is the whole point. It reminds

|| गङ्गां शरणं गच्छामि सर्वपापप्रणाशिनीम्। ||

I take refuge in Ganga, the destroyer of all sins.

A devotional mantra widely used in daily prayers, where the river Ganga is invoked

pilgrims that all structures, identities and achievements, no matter how impressive, are ultimately temporary. The Kumbh city is a ritual theatre of detachment. All those who dwell in it subconsciously internalize the transitory nature of life.

The temporary city can also be seen as a metaphor for cyclical time – a core tenet of Hindu cosmology. Just as the universe is created, sustained and eventually dissolved in a cosmic cycle (srishti, sthiti, pralaya), the Kumbh city mirrors this sacred rhythm. It is built (creation), lived in (sustained) and dismantled (dissolution), echoing the cosmic order on human scale.

|| आपः पुनन्तु पृथिवीं पृथिवी पूतुमा पुनातु माम्। ||

अथर्ववेद 18.4.14

जल पृथ्वी को पवित्र करे और यह शुद्ध पृथ्वी मुझे भी पवित्र करे।

From solitude towards salvation

AMRIT: AN ELIXIR OF THE IMMORTALS

When one sees all beings as the Self, where is delusion or sorrow?

|| ममैवांशो जीवलोके जीवभूतः सनातनः ||

Bhagvad Gita (Chapter 15, Verse 7)

A fragment of my own self becomes the eternal soul in beings.

Ever since a drop of amrit, the nectar of immortality, slipped through the fingers of the gods and landed here, Prayag has magnetized humanity. Generations have come here from across the land and beyond, not to find the drop but to remember the ocean it came from.

In the swirl of dust and conches, among naked sadhus and silent pilgrims, time folds in on itself, and the boundaries between the earthly and the divine dissolve. Every twelve years, the Kumbh becomes a mirror of the nation's soul. Amid saints and selfie sticks, trance and traffic, the thudding heart of India beats steadily. To come to the Kumbh is to walk into a myth.

The Sangam becomes an open temple, accessible to all. The sacred is not locked in architecture: there are no gates, no walls, no roof. It is just a shared moment. It suggests a radical idea: that sanctity does not need permanence, that the divine can arise wherever people gather with sincerity. The Kumbh Mela is illustrative of the transience of all things. It teaches the same truth that the river demonstrates every day: everything flows, nothing stays, and yet all things are eternal. Because all things are born of the eternal. The Kumbh also communicates a sense of destiny: you come to the Mela thinking that you are just a visitor. You leave knowing you were expected here. You are the centre. You are the whole point. You are amrit – eternal.

When thoughts dissolve like mist, when constellations whisper ancient tales, each star becomes a beacon, and each soul a voyager

|| यत् पिण्डे तत् ब्रह्माण्डे ||

As within the body, so in the universe.

ABOUT THE AUTHOR

Meenakshi Singh is an Indian Revenue Service (IRS) officer with over thirty-two years of distinguished service in the fields of finance, taxation, trade, industry and administration. She currently serves as the Principal Commissioner of Income Tax in Lucknow. She has previously served as the Commissioner of International Taxation and Commissioner of TDS in Delhi.

While on deputation to the India Trade Promotion Organisation, she represented India at several international forums across Australia, Japan, South Africa, Chile and other nations, promoting brand India on the global stage. She was also part of the core team behind the redevelopment of Pragati Maidan, a landmark national infrastructure project.

Singh has been the recipient of the Finance Minister's Award in recognition of her service to the taxpayers. An alumna of the Delhi University, she holds a postgraduate degree from the Delhi School of Economics and has a bachelor's degree in law. Beyond her civil service career, she is a passionate environmentalist and wildlife conservationist, and is deeply committed to the empowerment of women and children.

Photography is her creative calling, and her first exhibition, titled 'Taj Mahal: Through the Twilights of Time', was held at Bikaner House, New Delhi, in 2023. This body of work captured the changing moods of the stunning Taj across different seasons, its changing colours from dawn to dusk and its magic by moonlight.

This book marks her first published collection of photographs. It documents Maha Kumbh 2025, a sacred congregation that occurs every 144 years – a tribute to faith, humanity and celestial rhythm.